DISCOVERING DISCIPLESHIP

The teachings of Jesus about
Christian character

by
George Johnston
B.D., Ph.D., D.D., L.L.D.

with a study guide by
James Taylor

produced for
VENTURES IN MISSION
by Wood Lake Books, Inc.
Winfield, B.C.

Canadian Cataloguing in Publication Data

Johnston, George, 1913-
    Discovering discipleship

    Bibliography: p.
    ISBN 0-919599-09-5

    1. Christian life - 1960-
2. Jesus Christ - Teachings. I. Taylor,
James. II. Ventures in Mission. III Title.
BV4501.2.J64   248.4   C83-091172-3

Ron Cole/Berkeley Studio photo

First printing: April 1983
Second printing: September 1983
Printed and bound in Canada by
Friesen Printers
a Division of D. W. Friesen & Sons Ltd.,
Altona, Manitoba R0G 0B0
Canada

ISBN 0-919599-09-5

INTRODUCTION

For the early Christian writers, to be a Christian was to be a disciple of Jesus, accepting all of the obligations and responsibilities of the original disciples.

Today, increasing numbers of Christians are realizing that being Christian means more than simply accepting the name of Christ and attending church on a more or less regular basis. To be a Christian today also means being a disciple of Jesus.

In this book, Dr. George Johnston, former principal of United Theological College in Montreal and professor of New Testament at McGill University, examines what Jesus said about the qualities expected of his disciples. It is character that makes a disciple, not any abstract application of rules or doctrines in isolated situations.

Dr. Johnston's careful revelation of Jesus' authentic teachings about discipleship are accompanied in this book by six group-study sessions developed by James Taylor, the editor of Wood Lake Books. These sessions are designed to assist persons in congregations in coming to grips with Jesus' teachings about discipleship in their own lives and in their association with the larger church.

Where this book is being used for a study program, it is recommended that each participant have a copy to read and study before each session. Additional copies are available through all Canec book stores: in Edmonton, 7692 99th St., 432-7411; in Winnipeg, 120 Maryland St., 783-7927; in Toronto, 85 St. Clair Ave. E., 925-6597, and in Dieppe, N.B., 855-5212.

> In these pages, certain passages have been marked by vertical bars on both sides. These passages contain the more academic (and, for some, abstruse) aspects of biblical scholarship. For those with theological training or studious minds, these portions may be among the most valuable in the booklet. For others, however, these portions may be skipped over without missing Dr. Johnston's main theme.

It is not necessary to read the portions marked off with vertical bars in order to understand Jesus' teachings about discipleship.

over

continued

This study program has been produced for and in support of VENTURES IN MISSION, and its aim is the spiritual growth and renewal of the church. We hope that individuals and groups using this Bible study program will let us know about their experiences with it. Our address is:

VENTURES IN MISSION,
The United Church of Canada,
85 St. Clair Ave. E.,
Toronto, Ontario, M4T 1M8

VENTURES IN MISSION is grateful to George Johnston and Jim Taylor for producing and providing this Bible Study program on discipleship for the United Church of Canada.

Doug Shanks,
National Co-ordinator,
Information and Study,
VENTURES IN MISSION.

CONTENTS

over

SIX STUDY SESSIONS

DISCOVERING DISCIPLESHIP

The teachings of Jesus about Christian character

by George Johnston

I. THE WORD BECOMES FLESH

Who was Jesus?

The moral teaching of Jesus comes from a first-century Galilean Jewish religious leader. In the Gospels as we have them, this teaching is now intertwined with theological and devotional material that reflects what E. F. Scott in *The Fourth Gospel* called "the immediate practical needs of the early Church".

Jesus directed his message originally to Galilean and Judaean disciples and others in his own time and locale. The interpreter of that message today must beware therefore of simple transposition into the history and geography of any other group, including his own. Its immediate religious context seems to have been within a general expectation of a new age, the so-called "kingdom of God", when liberation, peace, prosperity and true piety would flourish again in the land of Israel, and perhaps throughout the world.

The teaching of Jesus still has much of value to say to men and women in the late twentieth century, but not because it was expressed in lucid, rationally argued general principles. As the middle-Eastern scholar Kenneth Bailey showed in his book *Poet and Peasant,* Jesus was more poet than philosopher. Furthermore, Jesus spoke out of a distinctly Jewish and middle-Eastern context. He presupposed the existence and to a large extent the moral authority of the *Torah,* God's revelation to Israel, recorded in his nation's scriptures. Biblical law governed the life of Israel,though it was interpreted with considerable differences by the Pharisees, Sadducees, Essenes and the general public of Jesus' time.

The ethical teaching of Jesus survived because scores of congregations rapidly developed in the Mediterranean area. People learned to hear in the gospel about this prophetic Galilean teacher nothing less than God's Word, a new revelation of God himself, and to discover in discipleship a faith to overcome the fear of death and the impotence of their moral life.

In word as well as act, indeed in his continuing "presence" within the churches, Jesus captured hearts. He brought new hope and remade lives by the power of his dying, by his own personal charm and grace, and by the spiritual penetration of his mind and the saintliness of his character. Disciples who had known him in the flesh were bound into profound communion with other disciples who adhered to him long after his death; the continuity between these two groups across the centuries must be appreciated. "Blessed are they who have come to believe, even though they have not seen me!" John quotes Jesus as saying (20:29).

This same Jesus is the living Lord of the Church today. Millions of people still affirm the spiritual power that flows from contact with him, through the sacraments and rites of religion, through the Gospels and their interpretation, and through the liberating effects of his teaching on motives, ambitions and self-criticism in their daily life. These are facts in the public domain. There is absolutely no need to demonstrate that his teaching remains "relevant".

What Jesus had to say about the value and quality of life, on what is virtuous and what is vicious, on what sort of behaviour should be expected of the truly humane person, was born out of his religion and theology.

One cannot begin to appreciate his judgments on character and virtue until one has assessed and understood what he meant by God, humanity, and destiny, and until the peculiar nature of his career has been perceived. He was neither politician nor schoolmaster. He was a prophet who came with a unique vision of God and God's activity in the history of Jews and Gentiles.

The literature on this subject is vast. One of the most recent and accessible books is *Jesus Means Life,* by Harold and Patricia Wells, a United Church of Canada study book for 1983 published by the Division of Communication and available at all Canec branches for $5.95.

Our Sources of Knowledge

The four gospels of the New Testament are virtually the only primary sources we possess for knowledge of Jesus' mission and message. For their own time and place they were unusual documents, in spite of any likenesses that may be detected between them and the "Lives" of other religious heroes and famous men in the Hellenistic world.

None of the gospels was written, probably, before A.D. 65 or later than A.D. 100. Critical scholars recognize today that each of the four Evangelists had a point of view and was more than a mere compiler of traditions—though in my judgment it goes too far to dignify each of them with the designation of "theologian". They each edited tradition stories and sources of many different kinds. To some extent, too, they must be read as authors in their own right.

Their writings can be examined and assessed in a number of ways. The literary methods of structural analysis have enriched their interpretation in recent years; this way of studying the gospels is now challenging the disciplines of historical analysis which have developed since the middle of the eighteenth century.

What one seeks to do both in historical and literary analysis is to reach behind the authors' editorial processes, to discover the real public ministry of Jesus and his authentic teaching. There are immense difficulties in the enterprise, so one must be careful not to claim too much and not to be dogmatic. The material is composite, and research cannot infallibly unravel it nor trace with complete success the authors' processes of selecting from, and transmitting, the traditions about Jesus.

The position adopted in this book is that one *can* isolate certain sayings of Jesus which appear in virtually identical form in Matthew and Luke, but which do not appear in Mark, John or any apocryphal gospel. They are denoted as Q, a code name given to a collection of sayings probably translated into Hellenistic Greek out of Jesus' own Aramaic speech.

We have no original Q manuscripts, so its existence is of course hypothetical. Nevertheless, a scholar such as P. Vassiliadis is so convinced that Q was a single written document that he even defines a list of passages within it.

Q has come down with some translation variants and some harmonizing (e.g. with Mark's sayings) and it may be wrong to imagine it as a single written document. What is utterly illegitimate is to enlarge Q by including in it any text that is found in only one of the gospels. By definition, a Q saying must be present in both Luke and Matthew. For convenience, I have usually cited it in Luke's version.

Mark, in my view, is a major source for Matthew and for Luke. I consider it incredible to think of him merely as an abbreviator of either Matthew or Luke, as some scholars (such as Griesbach and his disciples) have attempted to argue.

There remains, then, a body of teaching that is found only in Luke, but nowhere else, or only in Matthew. In identifying those passages, I have simply noted them as Matthew or Luke—those passages derived from a common source, I have prefixed, Q-Luke or Q-Matthew.

The Fourth Gospel too contains sayings of Jesus, though few of them correspond in form or substance with what is derived from the Synoptic Gospels of Matthew, Mark and Luke. In John, Jesus' teachings have been assembled in longish discourses that comprise what must be dubbed "Johannine theology". While Jesus' intent may be well represented in John, it is difficult, though not impossible, to find his authentic words in that Gospel.

Unfortunately there is still no consensus about criteria by which Jesus' authentic teaching can be recognized. My own working hypothesis is that form history and tradition history are helpful tools, but that classification by form has little bearing on a saying's credibility. Some stories told about Jesus are almost certainly the exaggeration of hero-worship, saint-worship, or of an incarnational Christology that makes him appear to be a divine magician. In the gospels he employs riddles, epigrams, parables, poems, apocalyptic predictions and even homilies. He used also a strange metaphoric I-form, found in his "I am..." statements. Most of these—"I am the bread of life...", "I am the light of the world..."—occur in

John.

Not all of these sayings can be accepted literally and uncritically for a variety of reasons, including internal consistency and adaptation to conditions of church life long after Jesus' time.

It is important also to note when a saying is current in one source only. In itself that demands caution, though of course a statistical argument is not always conclusive: a saying found only in Matthew, for example, may be fully in line with the message as a whole. Still, multiple attestation should give a certain amount of confidence. In other words, where later theological or ecclesiological additions are unlikely, support from a second source such as Q or Mark would provide significant evidence of authenticity.

The Theology Of Jesus

Jesus had a theology, and much of it was expressed in his parables.

He offered no philosophical arguments for the Being and nature of God. For him, God is the Covenant-Lord of Israel, creator and lord of the world, God of the patriarchs and of Moses—One who is real, alive, active, worthy of service.

Jesus seems to have considered himself heir to the Pentateuch, the prophets, and the Psalter of his people. In Mark 10:2-9 and in Matthew 5 he deliberately updates the historic teachings. But he does not take on this role uncritically. His God was no nationalist deity, even if there is evidence to indicate that Jesus confined his own mission to the borders of Israel.

Jesus' God is not remote and austere, but rather is a loving Father, *Abba,* one who is merciful, kind and forgiving as well as impartial and just. At the same time, this God is the Sovereign Lord of Israel and of all nations. As the living God he had revealed himself and his purposes to the prophets for their time, and to John the Baptist, the immediate predecessor of Jesus, described as "a very great one among those born of women'' (Q-Luke 7:28), and ultimately to Jesus himself (Q-Luke 10:21f.).

There is no reason to doubt that Jesus claimed to have been ''sent'' by God as his representative at a critical moment (a *Kairos*) in the history of Israel (Mark 1:15; compare John 5:43; 6:29). This vocation may have been proclaimed in Sonship language, whether as Son of Man or Son of God, but it should not, I think, be interpreted as a claim to Deity. The Father's Son is his representative or apostle, who speaks with authority (Mark 1:22).

The key to Jesus' theology, however, lies in Mark 1:15, which should be read alongside Q-Luke 11:20; Luke 17:20f.; and Matthew 11:12f./Luke 16:16, which are variants of a Q saying. Together they show that Jesus preached a decisive intervention of God. Expressed in conventional terms, ''the kingdom of God is near'' (or the like), was a reference to the long awaited Messianic Age when Israel's ''salvation'' would be realized. If one may still speak in this way, then the ethics of Jesus can be described as ''Kingdom ethics''.

This has been challenged by Earl Breech of Toronto in his ''Kingdom of God and the Parables of Jesus'', a lively contribution to *The Poetics of Faith*. Breech argues that the poet-prophet Jesus shattered with gentle humour the religious expectations of his contemporaries, but he did not shatter their world. Time did not come to an end, and the apocalyptic wonders foreseen by intertestamental dreamers did not come to pass. Hence, says Breech, Jesus did not ''proclaim the Kingdom of God'' as many New Testament scholars, following J. Weiss, Albert Schweitzer, R. Bultmann and C.H. Dodd, have held since 1892.

It is important not to misuse the concept of God's rule or kingship. We must get rid of ideas like empire, realm, or kingdom within which Jesus was to be the Viceroy or Sovereign, or the Prince. In Jesus' own time, the Essenes of the Qumran community, for example, looked for a Prince of Israel (*sar yisrael*) in the Messianic Age, as well as a Messianic Priest and perhaps also a Prophet like Moses. We need to remember that the inscription on the Cross, ''King of the Jews'', was not, after all, Jesus' choice of titles.

Yet the concept of God acting with royal power in and through a representative cannot be excised. God is not to be compared with Caesar or Herod. Paradoxically, God is most loving, gracious and humble. Jesus had new things to teach about the New Age when God would be served by people who understood God's will and methods. They were so new that they were misinterpreted and Jesus himself was proclaimed as King-Messiah, son of David (Luke 1:32; Acts 1:6).

The Duty Of Discipleship

Jesus' ethical teaching belongs intimately with his word about God's strange work. His is a theological ethic. That is, character, virtue and human relationships all depend on doing God's will. That was initially true for Jesus himself. By example and teaching, his ethic was directed to his pupils and apprentices (cf. Matthew 10:24f.).

The duty laid on Jesus, to represent the Father, became for them the duty to represent Jesus (Luke 10:16). This "apostolic impersonation" appears in negative and positive versions in an variety of sources, and it must be authentic to Jesus.

That may suggest that Jesus and his disciples formed a closed School, similar to the Academy or the Lyceum in Athens, but one should not press the analogy, for Jesus' gospel must be set fully within the framework of divine action inaugurating a new era. His ethic was not narrowly related to scholars. Nor was it a rule of life for a church. It was addressed, I believe, to everyone in Israel who was willing to listen; and it was not an "eschatological" ideal to be realized only in some divine realm beyond space and time. Jesus' demands fell on a particular situation and asked for response there and then.

It was a radically religious message that mercilessly exposed hidden lusts in the heart and the pretences even of the devout among his peers. The fact that Jesus attacked Jewish vices does not mean that he was anti-Semitic, and the fact that his followers recorded his words does not make them anti-Semitic either, whatever some contemporary scholars may say to that effect. The faults he exposed were human faults, equally common among Gentiles, and modern readers often find themselves being probed by the rigour of Jesus' sincerity and the sureness of his moral analysis.

His message can be profoundly disturbing, a penetrating provocative word from a teacher who inspired a remarkable devotion. It is alive with the spiritual dynamism that is proper to an exciting theology. For Jesus seems to have been utterly convinced that God is near and will finally be in complete control of human destiny. Evil will not triumph. The good is man's duty, and the will of God should be, could be, can be done in the land.

> Whether Matthew's editorial addition or not, this idea of "your will be done" (Matthew 6:10) fits the Lord's Prayer that longs for the Sanctification of the Name and for divine rescue from the tribulation (not "temptation") that may befall men and women before the ultimate victory of the truth.
>
> 1 Thess. 1:10; Mark 8:38 and Acts 3:19-21 and many other texts point to a primitive concept in the Church that there is to be an End (a *telos*, Mark 13:7), a Goal, when God's purposes will be fulfilled. Probably Jesus shared that idea, which may be called theological or eschatological. But one cannot at this distance in time define precisely Jesus' hopes, especially the view he took of the imminence of the End. It is essential to relate his teaching about advent and nearness to the then current desire for a new historical epoch for Israel and the nations, and to define his hope as part of his faith in a God who will accomplish the divine intention for mankind and the entire creation.

In what follows I shall be examining what kind of person it is who hears the Word of God in Jesus' gospel; what that person is to become as a servant of God and a representative of Jesus. We have to see how Jesus regards a disciple, because the New Testament writers who followed him defined Christian character in a real sense as "disciples of Jesus". I shall pay little attention to the ordering of society in the Mediterranean world of the first Christian century, though that environment needs always to be kept in mind. The point is *what it means to be Christian,* not what it means or meant to be a fully accredited or paid-up member of a church.

> For further reading on this subject, Hans Kung's *On Being a Christian* is a remarkable volume of great value, written from his own Catholic perspective. My purpose here is much more limited—an exposition of New Testament teaching by a professional biblical scholar, who happens to be a Protestant.
>
> Some excellent insights in terms of understanding the concepts of "Kingdom", "Servant", etc., can be found in *46 Images,* a daily devotional book published by the United Church in 1983.

II. THE CALL TO DISCIPLESHIP

For the purpose of this study it is unnecessary to produce a fully documented history of Jesus' career. I simply want to provide what seems to be a reasonable interpretation of his mission, during which he invited men and women to "follow".

The Turning Point

There are key texts in Mark, Q and Luke that suggest an atmosphere of exhilaration, urgency and crisis:

(1) Mark 1:15. After the arrest of John the Baptist, Jesus proclaimed that "The time (kairos) has reached its term and the Rule of God (i.e. God in person) has come near; turn again, therefore, believe this good news!" Galileans and Judaeans at that period in their history would have understood from such words that something momentous was being said.

(2) Luke 10:9, 11 (compare Matthew 10:7). On their mission, the Seventy (or Seventy-two) were to insist that God's Rule had drawn near: "God is at the door!"

Q-Luke 11:20. Jesus said, "If it is by God's finger (Matthew 12:28 has 'spirit') that I am exorcising demons, then God in his saving power has fallen upon you." God is present as the Healer of Israel in the person of the healing Jesus.

Q-Luke 16:16. "The Law and the Prophets (lasted) until John; since then, God's Rule is being gospelled, and every one lays violent hands on it." This is a difficult saying, and Matthew's parallel differs markedly.

It could be argued that the note of advent or imminence is due to the theological tendency of the compiler or editor of Q, as R.A. Edwards theorized in *The Theology of Q*. But I am not convinced that this has been demonstrated. Jesus seems to have been certain that his entry on the scene ushered in a new era because he brought God's power with him.

(3) Luke 17:20f. "...look you! God's Rule is within reach" (not,

within you; nor, probably, *among you,* though the latter is possible). There was joy because great and wonderful things were taking place; there was also a sense of crisis and an expectation of more to come in the immediate future. Luke 11:2 advises disciples to pray, "Father, may your Rule come", and near the end of the public ministry Jesus warns his friends to stay awake and be on the look-out (Mark 13:32-37; Matthew 25:1-13).

The phrase "Rule of God" does less than justice to Jesus' meaning. One may paraphrase "Rule of God" as follows: "The long expected, sovereign, redemptive activity of Yahweh (God), at a crisis of the ages, on behalf of his covenant People, Israel."

Moments Of Crisis

This turning-point should not, I suggest, be defined in apocalyptic terms as "the end of the world" or "the end of history", though admittedly an element of apocalyptic ideas may have lingered in the authentic teaching of Jesus. Essentially, the gospel spoke of a new epoch, made possible by God but always dependent in a sense on Israel's response. Jesus was the heir to ancient hopes of a Messiah.

These can be traced back to the ancient hope of a Davidic king (2 Sam. 7:14-16; Isa. 9:6f.); the exilic assurance of a restored monarchy in the prophecies of Ezekiel 37:1f., 21-28; the King-Priest combination of Zechariah 6:9-14; and the visionary predictions ascribed to Daniel at the beginning of the Maccabaean period (Dan. 7:9-14; 9:24-27). In the Daniel passage the man-like figure, the "Son of Man", may stand for royal Israel, the People of God, or for the archangel Michael, the Guardian of Israel, or perhaps for both, in typically Semitic fashion. Royal hopes persisted among the pietists of the second century B.C. (compare the Psalms of Solomon 17). Princely and priestly ideas were current among the Qumran Essenes, but other elements were included, notably that of the Prophet like Moses of Deuteronomy 18:15 (the Qumran *Testimonia;* compare Acts 3:22; John 6:14f.).

> There were in fact a host of conflicting Messianic ideas floating in the air at the end of Herod's reign when Jesus was born. One must be very cautious about tracing the lineage through Old Testament texts.

It is doubtful indeed whether Jesus' views should be called Messianic except in broad terms, for he showed no interest in becoming a Davidic King. He had no qualifications to be High Priest. But he might have aspired to be an innovative Prophet and a greater Moses. For he seems to have been certain that the Spirit of God was active in and through him, however little he actually said to that effect (compare Q-Luke 11:20 with Exod. 8:19; Mark 3:29f.).

One could say that as healer, teacher and prophet Jesus was the human presence of the divine spirit; what he taught about the character of his disciples emerged from the context of the vocation he had accepted as the Servant of the Lord.

He summoned an inner group to become healers, teachers and preachers like himself, presumably in the power of that same divine Spirit (Mark 6:7-13 and parallels). Jesus is the *One whom God sent,* and these disciples are *Those whom Jesus sent;* hence, to receive Jesus is to welcome God; and to welcome a disciple is to receive Jesus...and God also. This powerful doctrine is attested to by sufficient independent versions to be considered fully authentic (see Mark 9:37; Luke 10:16; Matthew 10:40; John 13:20, 17:18, and 20:21).

Urgency in responding is clear from Luke 13:1-5. Nothing should be allowed to interfere with the chance of entering the new age. If necessary, things that offend must be ruthlessly excised (Mark 9:43-47). If a person could stumble on treasure hidden in a field and, unscrupulously, get possession of it, how much more should Jesus' listeners emulate that single-mindedness! If a merchant trading in pearls might sell his entire stock in order to acquire a single pearl of surpassing value, how much more should those who could see what Jesus meant concentrate on God and his business, do the mad thing, sell all, do anything except lose the opportunity of a lifetime! For God, or God's new age, is like treasure and like a pearl that cannot be priced (Matthew 13:44-6).

A similar sense of urgency appears in Q-Matthew 5:25f., "come to terms with your accuser before you reach the court", and Luke 12:16-21, where God may require a man's life any night in the week.

Pearl? treasure? Yes, because for Jesus God must be conceived as *Abba,* Father, the Lord of infinite grace. Jesus subverted some current ideas about God and therefore about the just life, about goodness, about the character appropriate to worshippers. His teaching instrument for teasing this message into the minds of his listeners was the parable. His parables sometimes shock one into new awareness. Sometimes they are very homely and natural, yet always they point to the extraordinary, the eternal, the divine in their midst.

By Personal Example

Jesus' own life is the proof that his ethic belonged inextricably to his doctrine. The teaching of Mark 12:29-31, for example, must have found its home first in Jesus' own personality before he could have dared to pronounce on the heart and soul of God's revelation in the written *Torah.*

With fortitude and an obedient heart he left his home and put his head into Herod's noose, the Herod who had dealt so summarily with John the Baptist. Before long Jesus too had to reckon with an opposition that intended his death.

It appears that disciples were to follow him on the same road, and not everyone was ready to do so. To a wealthy aspirant Jesus said, "You lack one thing"; you must sell everything and come and walk with me, taking God into your life as a Presence to be adored and served (Mark 10:17-22; cf. 12:34). A single step and that man would have been into the new age. Riches, however, choked the response of obedience. So God remained at the door; the new age (the "Kingdom") had yet to be entered (Mark 10:25).

Another barrier to discipleship resided in the religious leadership and its piety. The Pharisees who along with others rejected Jesus were not scoundrels. They were among the best people that ever lived by the directives of a religious system. However, even after allowing for colouring by later Church-Synagogue debate and enmity, one must see Jesus as rebuking humbugs who preached and did not practise. By contrast, it is not only Christian bias that estimates Jesus as a preacher who in sincerity practised what he taught.

The Challenge

To appreciate more precisely the sort of persons who responded to Jesus, a tale may be married to an encounter.

The *encounter* is described in Luke 19:1-10. It was with Zacchaeus, a toll collector in Jericho who had a bad reputation and almost no friends. The result of his meeting with Jesus, who had invited himself to be his guest, may seem incredible and it is not fully explained in the narrative. He turned over half of his possessions to the poor and offered to make restitution fourfold to those whom he had defrauded.

For Zacchaeus, honesty had broken into his life.

For Zacchaeus, repentance became real, the result of God's presence in Jesus. If Abraham is "the father of the faithful", then Zacchaeus became "a son of Abraham" (Luke 19:9; compare Luke 13:16, Gal. 3:6-9; Romans 4:11b-16). Ancient promises had come true! This turn-around was also a liberation, and presumably the early Church knew how well Zacchaeus had kept his promise. He was the kind of person a Christian should be.

The *tale* that goes with the encounter is recorded in Luke 18:9-14. Zacchaeus might have provided material for it.

A Pharisee went up to the Temple to pray. A toll collector also went up, for the same purpose.

At once the hearer expects that God will listen to the virtuous man but pay no attention to the rascal. But the good man forgot the duty written for him in Leviticus 19:18 and the rest of that remarkable chapter. He despised his neighbour and thus forfeited his place before God. "He prayed with himself,"—a shocking commentary.

Meanwhile the tax-man stood far off, as if distance from the holy house should symbolize his separation from God's awful purity. He cried for mercy, and mercy is what he got.

A shocking state of affairs! Scoundrel he may have been, but now he could go home to his wife and children and his neighbours "justified", that is, forgiven and accepted; whereas the good man took his piety home none the better, for he had missed God by not recognizing the tax-man as a neighbour given to him by God.

By such words and deeds, then, Jesus challenged people and brought them hope.

The words were not set down verbatim nor did they become regulations, no doubt because Jesus had had no intention of bequeathing any sort of canon law to his disciples. Presumably his disciples understood this intention, for Matthew and Luke showed no compunction about altering to their own purposes the words of Jesus they found in Mark. Moreover, codification and regulation sit ill with a theology of the loving Father; they inhibit freedom. It was because faith in the Father was a kind of loving that is also imposed its own more commanding obligations, going far beyond convention and prudence. A spirit was passed on to enable women and men to exercise spiritual liberty in imaginative ways.

The moral teaching of Jesus, then, is no system of principles, precedents and examples for the discipline of a new cult. Rather, as Augustine once put it, one is to love God and do what one likes.

III. THE CHARACTER OF THE DISCIPLE

Vision And Insight

The early Church was preoccupied with the mystery of why some accepted Jesus' challenge and entered the new age, while others rejected it and brought about his death. A prophecy that had come true was frequently quoted from Isaiah 6:9f:

"Go, and say to this people,
'Hear and hear again, but do not understand;
see and see again, but do not perceive'.
Make the heart of this people gross,
its ears dull;
shut its eyes,
so that it will not see with its eyes,
hear with its ears,
understand with its heart,

(From the *Jerusalem Bible;* compare Jeremiah 5:21; Mark 4:12; Matthew 13:13-15; Luke 8:9f.; John 12:40; and Acts 28:26;27.)

Prophets like Jesus could not "reveal" God by making him visible to ordinary sight, nor could they communicate "the Word of God" by making it literally audible. Yet the Church insisted from the beginning that as "Son" Jesus had provided a personal exegesis or unfolding of the nature of God. This is the meaning of John 1:18, where Jesus is the *Logos* of God incarnate.

Whatever the idiom employed, the assumption was made that truth from God can indeed break through into human understanding, that light can dawn on a receptive spirit, that the divine mystery, while always beyond definition and explanation, is apprehended in reality. Jesus was a prophet in that tradition, and his disciple was anyone who was open to see and hear through him what "comes" from the Beyond.

As we have seen, relatively few responded affirmatively to Jesus. If we can trust the records, which do not conceal the evidence, even his closest friends were obtuse right to the end (Mark 8:17f.). They had the utmost difficulty in comprehending that the Rule of the Father, the impact of God's new age in its thrust into the present, had to mean the reversal of accepted ideas about Israel's future, whether associated with an Exodus Commander-in-chief, or a Prince, or a Prophet (compare Mark 11:27-33, 12:35-37). Mark 10:35f. makes clear that one who aspires to greatness must learn to serve—and forget about reputation! In God's new age the first are last and the meek inherit the land. This shocking reversal lies at the heart of Jesus' gospel.

Yet, as was claimed above, the Jesus-event was noted by Jesus himself as a time of divine presence and action to redeem and reveal. Independent traditions can be cited to this effect. There is the beatitude for disciples (Q-Luke 10:23f.): Blessed are the eyes which see what you see! For I tell you that many prophets and kings desired to see what you see, yet did not see it; and to hear what you are hearing, yet did not hear it.

> Several other Q sayings might be added, but I simply refer to them: Luke 7:22f. (alluding apparently to Isaiah 29:18f.; 35:4b-6; 61:1-3, 10f.); Matthew 6:22f., Luke 6:39; and the variants at Matthew 16:28 and Luke 12:54-56.

People with a diseased eye could not perceive the true significance of Jesus' mission.

Luke makes this point again in 17:20f.: "The Rule of God is not something to be gazed at. You can't say, 'Look, it's here!' or, 'Look, it's there!' "

The question Jesus put to listeners was, "Can you really see, that is, perceive the hidden reality?" Smug and careless folk were not likely to see, and what a great darkness comes if the eye is unsound and the organs of true vision are atrophied!

Spiritual comprehension may also be referred to in terms of "hearing", again in Mark, Q and Luke sayings:

Mark 4:9, 23, "He who has ears to hear, let him hear!"

In Q-Luke 6:46-49, hearing is an act of obedience, not a mere mechanical response. Fateful consequences flow from what one does with a prophetic word—"building on rock or building on sand".

Luke 16:29, "Let them attend to Moses and the prophets", means, simply, listen to the Word of God in scripture. (Verses 30f. are probably editorial additions.)

Much of this teaching was conveyed in parables which, as T.W. Manson said in *The Teaching of Jesus,* were instruments for confrontation with God. J.D. Crossan in *The Dark Interval* makes a similar point: they "are stories which shatter the deep structure of our accepted world and thereby render clear and evident to us the relativity of story itself. They remove our defences and make us vulnerable to God. It is only in such experiences that God can touch us, and only in such moments does the Kingdom of God arrive."

When willing obedience results from vision and hearing, it is understood that there is no merit in it: "When you have done all that is commanded, say, 'We are unworthy servants; we have done only what it was our duty to do' " (Luke 17:10).

There is however a reward, the knowledge of God's will. That brings with it a demand for other qualities like integrity, fidelity, an overflowing charity, and a family spirit (Mark 3:35).

Obedience

So important is this theme of obedience that further space must be devoted to it. "May your will be done" may have been deliberately added by Matthew to what we now call the Lord's Prayer, the pattern prayer in Matthew 6:10, on the analogy of Jesus' own petition in Gethsemane (Mark 14:36). The phrase is missing in Luke's version (11:2-4).

It was inevitable, in the Jewish context of Jesus' ministry, that discussion of the whole duty of a disciple as it related to God's will should proceed from biblical interpretation. Thus in Mark 12:28-34 a scribe enquired, "Which commandment is the first of all?" and Jesus replied by citing the *Shema'* (Deuteronomy 6:4) in combination with Deuteronomy 6:5 and Leviticus 19:18. Men and women are to love God wholeheartedly and to love neighbours wholeheartedly too.

Other Jewish teachers had already brought this double Command-ment to the forefront. Hillel and Akiba singled out Leviticus 19:18 as the "weightiest" of all the rules in *Torah,* without setting aside or disregarding as obsolete a single one of the host of regulations. Jesus went beyond this, making these two scriptural injunctions superior to all others.

> Luke 10:25-28 may come from an independent tradition. Here a lawyer tested Jesus with the question, "What am I to do in order to inherit eternal life?" (compare Mark 10:17). Such a man would have been expert in biblical lore and exegesis, so he is invited to answer his own question. He then cites Deut. 6:5 and Lev. 19:18, but not the *Shema'.*

In this summary, love for God, i.e. obedience, is to include devotion of *soul, heart* and *strength,* terms which are best rendered as *life, mind* and *possessions.* God is so important that one must be prepared to sacrifice everything, even life itself, in his service.

> If Jesus really meant to define the second rule ("love your neighbour") as a true correlate of the first, then one is indeed called to an impossible ethic! A variant that is perhaps narrower than Jesus' original wording appears at John 15:13, "Greater love has no man than this, that a man lay down his life for his friends".

According to Q-Luke 6:27,28,35, and Q-Matthew 5:44f., Jesus went still farther in requiring disciples *to love their enemies and pray for their persecutors.* Again one has to admit that the basis of this had been laid down in Leviticus 19:33f.: "Do not mistreat aliens who are living in your land. Treat them as you would a fellow Israelite, and love them as you love yourselves"(*Good News Bible*). But it was Jesus who pushed this to its limits, as an original contribution to ethics.

Thus in his theology and moral teaching Jesus was not out of line with the spirit of the *Torah:* In one way he was more rigorous; in others, far simpler. He was not a legalist, for he understood the God-humanity relationship in Father-child terms. He insisted that human life stands under the power, the wisdom, the purpose of the Creator.

Moral obligation—the duty to think straight, to act from pure motives, to fulfill a god-given destiny as persons (to use language appropriate to modern ethical theory) sprang inevitably from the worship of God, who is ultimate and inescapable.

Emily Carr, the Canadian painter, was seeking after this as she counselled herself, in her *Journals:* "Desire only that the consciousness of the presence of God may show and speak, not as accomplished by you, not as your work, not as having anything to do with you, but being only a reminder and an explainer of the manifested Father, the Christ."

For Jesus, one meaning of loving God wholeheartedly was that a disciple must always be one *who lets God be God.*

God is the Lord over all life, not an idol, not a human contrivance and convenience. Meeting with God, therefore, even as *Abba,* is always a meeting with conscience, with the demands of the right, the good and the true. Yet as *Abba,* God cares for all his works, and not least for human persons (Matthew 12:12a, confirmed by Q-Luke 12:7, 24).

A God like this is not the impassible Deity of philosophers. For Jesus, loving God means preferring God's honour and will above everything and everyone else. It does not mean being a diligent participant at cultic celebrations, nor being a formally dutiful keeper of regulations. As lover, one may have to break certain supposed divine laws or to fulfil them only in a very paradoxical way, as Jesus demonstrated in his own attitude to Sabbath rules (Mark 2:23-3:6; Matthew 12:7; compare Hosea 6:6).

The primary responsibility of a disciple, then, is a passionate commitment to the will of God as the Father whose rights are absolute.

Trust

In the magnificent prose poem in Q-Luke 12:22-31 and Q-Matthew 6:25-33, Jesus instructs his disciples about the importance of an almost childlike trust in God.

Not anxiety, he says, but trust is proper to the children of a God whose presence and joys are offered as gifts (Luke 12:32). Nevertheless, childlike trust belongs with insistent audacity, for the reality disciples confront is the Eternal God. They must seek, want, and press on to enter God's new age. "Keep on asking, keep on seeking, keep on knocking," said Jesus (Q-Luke 11:9). The spiritual benefits of God's rule are not to be had (so to speak) by timid requests or by casual response (compare Luke 18:1-8).

To this requirement we may add the narrative of the children welcomed, embraced and blessed (Mark 10:13-16). There is no need to doubt the authenticity of both sayings: "Let the children come to me... you must receive God's rule like a little child." Of course children belong in the world of God and in his new age. In the Jewish community they were welcomed as God's gifts and at once taken into the covenant. They grew up to learn and accept their covenant obligations. It was not to be different in the Jesus-community.

Yet how significant it was that a disciple had to be childlike in receiving the gift of the new order of life.

Loyalty

At the same time, fatherliness did not exclude from God the prerogatives of sovereignty. Hence an undivided loyalty was required of the disciple: "No servant can serve two masters... You cannot serve God and mammon" (Q-Luke 16:13). We may relate to this the clever argument in Mark 12:17, "Render to Caesar what is his, and to God also what belongs to him." This should not be taken to mean that Jesus recognized spheres of influence or national governments. Nothing in his teaching, as it has survived, suggests that he paid much attention to political issues, so one must be very cautious about drawing larger inferences from an isolated text—rather, it should be tasted with a salty dose of humour. Certainly the early Church knew well its duty to prefer God to Caesar (Acts 5:29; Revelation 2:13), though both Paul and Peter admitted to Caesar a special place as a source of order and a hedge against anarchy (Romans 13:1-7; 1 Peter 2:17).

Humility

In terms of character, nothing seems to be of more importance than that a disciple should be humble.

"Come to me... and I will refresh you. Take my yoke upon you and learn of me; for I am gentle and meek-hearted..." (Matthew 11:28f.) rings true to the personality of Jesus.

There may be in it, as we now have it, literary reminiscence of sayings in the Jewish tradition about the personified Wisdom of God. As a worshipper fed on Psalms like the 37th, 73rd, 112th, and 131st, Jesus would certainly have been familiar with Jewish Wisdom literature. But that need not cause us to be skeptical about Jesus' ability to use it about himself as God's representative to Israel. Jesus was an Israelite in whom genuine humility was wedded with an astonishing assurance that he spoke for God.

The example set by Jesus holds equally true for those who would be disciples. Hence "a disciple is not above his teacher, nor a servant above his master. It is enough for the disciple to be like his teacher, and the servant like his master" (Matthew 10:24-25a). Q-Luke 14:11 gives, "For everyone who exalts himself will be humbled, and he who humbles himself will be exalted", and it is supported by Mark's parallels, "Whoever would be great among you must be your servant..." (10:44; compare 9:35). Of Jesus himself it is true (in a saying where an original "I" has apparently been replaced by "the Son of Man") that, "I came not to be served but to serve" (Mark 10:45a). We have to deal here with an authentic historical person, not with a concoction of the gospel writers and the Church.

Humble disciples of a humble Teacher—it cannot be too much emphasized that the gospels insist on the Imitation of Jesus in the moral life and the service of God. There is nothing marginal about this in New Testament thought, provided that "imitation" is not interpreted in literal terms. Jesus invited friends to share his work and perform it *in the same spirit.*

But in the final analysis, it is God who is the Example to be followed: "Love your enemies... and then your reward will be plentiful, for you will be the children ('sons' in the original) of the Most High who is decent to ingrates and to scoundrels" (Luke 6:35).

To be Godlike becomes the supreme reward and indeed the final destiny of women and men created in God's own image, as Genesis had taught.

Forgiveness And Caring

Matthew's version of the Sermon on the Mount (5:19f., 21-24, 27f., 33-41) includes a number of significant elements of discipleship. They may be grouped as: obedience; a piety that excels the best in Judaism; and a contrast between Jesus' requirements and those of teachers in the olden time.

Six times in Matthew 5:21-48 there is a formula, "you have heard that it was said... But I say to you..." This section shows the marks of careful editing by Matthew or a predecessor. I am inclined to hold, however, that Jesus did use such a formula as a sign of his authoritative reinterpretation of God's will. At this point we need to postulate a creative mind as the source for ethical teaching that ranks amongst the most profound in religious history. The mind of Jesus of Nazareth is the obvious and the best candidate.

George D. Kilpatrick in *The Origins of the Gospel according to Saint Matthew* argues that a peculiar documentary source lies behind Matt. 5:17-6:18. He believes that 5:19f., about those commandments that must not be relaxed, refers to the *new* commandments of the age inaugurated by Jesus, rather than the mass of *Torah* rules and their commentaries.

In that case 5:19f. may have a parallel in the word about binding and loosing in Matthew 16:19.

An example of ecclesiastical relaxation by late first century Christians is Matthew 5:32 (and 19:9), where divorce was permitted on the single ground of fornication, contrary to the original teaching of Mark 10:5-9 where divorce seems to be totally forbidden.

Exposing The Motivations

Not everything, then, in Matthew 5:21f. or in the rest of the Sermon on the Mount can be positively attributed to Jesus. The original teaching of Jesus may be detected in the following:

(a) that anger and refusal to be reconciled with a neighbour or a kinsman in the community are just as forbidden as murder itself.

(b) that a lustful look can be every bit as sinful as the act of adultery. (Of course it is an outrageous saying, but it is probably fully authentic!)

(c) that one's language should be direct, simple and believable without benefit of oaths. This is entirely consistent with Jesus' message about personal relationships.

(d) that revenge is intolerable. Disciples must be willing to take an insult, or share clothes with would-be borrowers. All these are forms of the Golden Rule in practice.

Q-Luke 6:29a, the instruction to "turn the other cheek", may also be noted here. It is a text that too often has been regarded as a prosaic law of personal conduct and/or pressed into service as warrant for total pacifism. It is rather a pointer to the spirit of non-aggression advocated by Jesus. A disciple is one who has learned not to stand on his own rights.

(e) that loving a kinsman or neighbour must be extended to loving those who are hostile, by caring for their interests and showing them goodwill. It is right to care for those who cannot repay a kindness.

In each case an older Jewish rule stands, but Jesus exposes its deeper significance by pointing to motivations that govern character and lead to transgressions. In the world of the God who is Holy Father, love at its most unselfish and uncalculating creates moral demands even more rigorous than those of the *Torah* and of the Pharisaic traditions.

It is less likely that Matthew 5:20 is authentic: "unless your virtue goes far deeper than that of the scribes and Pharisees, you will certainly not enter into the kingdom of heaven''. According to Jesus, such an entrance is never a *reward* for good deeds, for righteousness or virtue done in conformity to Law. Penitent men and women would be received into the favour of God in spite of their demerits: ''I did not come to call the virtuous but sinners'' (Mark 2:17; compare Luke 15:1f.). (Yet it had to be true that, once in, they should never again be prodigals. As Luke 7:36f. makes clear, those who have been forgiven much will go on to love much, out of sheer joy and gratitude.)

Of course Jesus did not mean that a right response to God could come only from moral rotters. The meek and childlike can perceive and welcome the presence of God and the advent of his new age. So a good character could precede and transform *advent* into *arrival,* as in the case of old saints like Anna and Simeon, and perhaps of Mary and Joseph too.

Still, it is important to the theology of Jesus that entry into God's new world must effect a new character in his disciples, as subjects of the heavenly King, children of the holy Father.

Carved In Stone?

From a similar vantage point, one must ask whether the commandments of Jesus were delivered as obligations perpetually binding on disciples. The early Church did, to some extent, picture its Lord as a greater Moses. Yet Jesus made no such claim, and makes no such impression in the authentic teaching. He brought spiritual freedom, not a yoke to tie up the future. Accordingly, one must warn against any wooden application of even the statements that I have considered to be authentic.

Jesus' ethic, as preserved in our edited versions, does not deal with every important issue in human affairs; but those who seek to follow him as disciples are obliged to deal with every issue in his spirit, judging by his wisdom.

Accordingly, in relation to those statements above which summarize his original teaching in Matthew's sermon, we should remember that:

(a) There may be honest differences of opinion among friends.

(b) Amorous impulses are God-given and natural; the joys and laughter of a healthy sexuality are not to be banished by a rigid puritanism, nor can celibacy be elevated above the state of marriage. However legitimate be the lessons of the Genesis story of the Fall, it was God who invented the sexual relationship. Besides procreation, it has the function of sustaining the psychological health of males and females. The message of Jesus is that every such relationship should be governed by the rule of wholehearted caring and a love that is radiant with the purity and joy of God. Adultery is not condoned, because it destroys the union of persons in love.

(c) Simple speech is not the speech of simpletons. Jesus himself adorned his talking and teaching with puns, poems and humour, as re-translation into Aramaic has shown.

(d) Though individual retaliation was forbidden, this may not be applicable to the larger dimensions of complex social organizations. The weak have to be defended against the bullies; the order of society depends on some sort of enforcement, if only because people do not behave as brothers and sisters whose delight is to care for one another, as God cares.

(e) The requirement to care even for those who are hostile is a glorious saying which is also alarming, because it touches the most sensitive area of the conscience. In the world as it is, offences must come. Only the miraculous power of God operative in their inner life can enable people to forgive as they hope to be forgiven, to show mercy because they have received mercy, to exercise an unlimited patience ("to seventy-times seven") and to care about the welfare of enemies.

Jesus may have said this kind of thing on many occasions: Mark 11:25; Luke 6:37; Q-Luke 11:3-4; 17:3-4 (compare Matthew 18:15, 22); and Matthew 5:24; 18:23-34.

Without Exceptions

The need for forbearance was frequently emphasized by Jesus.

In Matthew 6:15 and 18:35 there is a warning about the spiritual peril in an unforgiving attitude, and it lurks also in the second half of the parable about Two Lost Sons in Luke 15:11f. Without such readiness to forgive, worship is formal, empty and useless (Matthew 5:23f.). Those who erect sullen selfish barriers to exclude neighbours from their caring can repel the love of God and keep themselves standing at the gate outside the new age. No more attractive or challenging example of what Jesus meant by neighbourly-love has ever been given, it is commonly held, than in the story of the Good Samaritan (Luke 10:29-37).

Almost certainly Luke is responsible for associating this story with Jesus' meeting a scribe or lawyer. Let us therefore first look at it separated from Luke's context.

Taken by itself, as has sometimes been noticed in recent studies, the story can be read from the point of view of the victim in the ditch who learned (and therefore teaches) some shocking lessons: help came *from an unexpected source,* indeed *from an alien source,* and *it came in overflowing measure of generosity.*

J.D Crossan should be quoted from his book *The Dark Interval:* "The hearer must not be able to shrug it off by saying: No Samaritan would act that way! He must feel instead: I have just seen the wine and the oil, the donkey, and the inn. I have just seen the two denarii exchange hands and I have just heard the Samaritan discuss the situation with the innkeeper... Whether one's mind reacts properly or not, the Good Samaritan ('the good terrorist', today?) is an attack on the structure of expectation and not a story which indicates assistance to those in distress although, of course, it takes it absolutely for granted that assistance is required in such a case."

In my judgment, however, this interpretation does not fully disclose the radically new word being said in this parable to a Jewish audience. The point is precisely that it was *a despised alien who fulfilled the will of God* stated in Jewish scripture (Leviticus 19:18), and who went two miles and more to help a foreigner (Matthew 5:41). This alien fellow (fictional indeed) must have stunned hearers, as he stuns readers, into some fresh comprehension of what Leviticus 19:18 imposes: there are to be no exceptions, no careful calculation of the kind recommended in *Situation Ethics,* no hesitation.

The Overriding Theme

Finally we come to the Golden Rule: "As you wish that men would do to you, do so to them" (Q-Luke 6:31).

In a negative form, scholars often remind us, there are many parallels to this: in Hillel according to *TB Shab.* 32a; Tobit 4:15; Philo according to Eusebius's *Praep. Evang.* VIII, 7. In his commentary on Luke, J.M. Creed cited also Isocrates, the Greek orator, *Nicodes* 49, 61, and the *Analects* of Confucius (XV, 23; cf. Acts 15:29, and *Didache* 1:2).

It seems to have become commonplace in contemporary scholarship to insist that the Golden Rule is old hat and of no importance. Dihle in *Die Goldene Regel,* even regards *Nicodes* 49 as a positive statement of the rule to look after a neighbour, and this is accepted by Victor Furnish in *The Love Command in the New Testament.*

Jacob Bernays, however, denied that Isocrates viewed the rule as a principle to be applied generally in human behaviour. And Israel Abrahams argued that "it is at least a tenable theory that the negative Rule goes deeper into the heart of the problem (i.e. of human weakness in the face of evil)."

Rudolf Bultmann in *The History of the Synoptic Tradition* goes farther: "It is a piece of self-deception to suppose that the positive form of the rule is characteristic for Jesus, in distinction from the attested negative form among the Rabbis. The positive form is purely accidental, for whether it be given positive or negative formulation the saying, as an individual utterance, gives moral expression to a naif egoism."

Others describe it as a calculating justice, a piece of Greek folk wisdom adopted by Judaism and then by Christianity, but argue that it must not be employed as an epitome of Jesus' original teaching.

I dissent very strongly from all of this.

The Golden Rule was no isolated utterance; it belongs with the first and great commandment and the theology of God as the *Abba* of all children. Hence, what is done to others is not to be done out of prudence or self-interest, if it is faithful to the spirit of the love ethic. The negative form of the Golden Rule, as found in other cultures and traditions—"do not do to others what you would not want them to do to you"—is a calculating piece of prudence which cannot be reconciled with Jesus' shocking emphasis on the love that gives all.

Disciples of Jesus were required to care for neighbours *without qualification*. The negative form does not oblige them to care for an enemy, to bless a persecutor, to live at peace and leave all vengeance to God, to feed the hungry, clothe the naked, visit the sick and the prisoner, suffer with the victims of torture and work for their liberation, and so to overcome evil with good, as St. Paul put it in an inspired comment (Romans 12:14-21).

By giving Jesus credit for inspiring a quality of caring that pushes beyond all limits, one need not deny to Greeks or Chinese or Jews or anyone else their own glimpses of the truth and their own partial obedience. Indeed, disciples of Jesus themselves show only a partial obedience.

Purity Of Heart

One further element of the character of a disciple remains to be discussed, namely purity of heart and the virtue appropriate to it.

The first passage needing to be considered is Mark 7:14-23, and in particular verse 15: "There is nothing that enters into a person from outside that can make him unclean. Rather, it is what proceeds from him that renders a person unclean."

Verse 16 about ears to hear should probably be omitted, as several modern versions do. Verse 19c, "thus he declared all foods clean", is an editorial embellishment, to be compared with Acts 10:14f. Verses 17-19a, in typical Marcan fashion, offer an explanatory comment in the light of the question posed at 7:5, "Why do your disciples not live according to the tradition of the elders?" What comes in, says the comment affects the stomach, not the heart. Now, it is not impossible that Verses 17-19 convey at least in part an authentic explanation of his own riddle by Jesus, for they are not alien to his mind and practice. Ritual washing (compare Leviticus 22:1-9) does not get at the basic need for spiritual cleanness, and Psalm 51:6, 10 as well as the Qumran *Manual of Discipline* (IQS 3:6-8) can be adduced in support. Verse 20 is merely a repetition of 15b. Verses 21-23 resemble a Table of Virtues and Vices of the kind familiar from Aristotle, Hellenistic ethics, Qumran, and early Christian letters. In itself the catalogue is not objectionable and we can find parallels in other teachings of Jesus: e.g., Luke 12:15 on covetousness; Luke 15:28-32 on anger; Matthew 5:22 also on anger; Luke 18:10-14 on pride; and Q-Luke 17:1f. on the wickedness of incitement to sin.

The result of radical literary analysis is that we have in Mark 7 a saying that may well be authentic—to estimate personal uncleanness, the heart must be searched. Purity of heart is essential to a disciple.

A significant passage comes from the Q tradition, Q-Luke 6:43-45, that good fruit comes from a healthy tree and bad fruit from a diseased one. Matthew refers this to true and false prophets (Matthew 7:17f.),whereas Luke set it within a series of paragraphs about sincerity and hypocrisy in disciples. Matthew picks it up a second time (12:34b, 35) just after a warning about slandering the Son of Man: every careless word must be accounted for at the Last Judgment.

Out of these references, two authentic statements can be uncovered. The first is a form of the earlier word in Mark: what a disciple says will reflect what is in his heart. The second is: as a tree is known by its fruit, so a good man can be known by the good he performs and a wicked man by wicked deeds. Motives are not left hanging in the air: actions also count.

The insight is very simple, and many people may be well aware of it. But Jesus takes it at the most serious level and by so doing displays an almost terrifying moral insight. Piety must conform to the character of the God who is worshipped; behaviour must fit the goodness of the same God. God requires sincerity and purity of heart (compare Psalm 24:4). The spring of the act lies in the secret self (compare Matthew 5:20f.).

How can such a standard possibly be satisfied?

A clue to Jesus' answer will be found in Mark 13:11 and the parallels at Q-Luke 12:11f. and Q-Matthew 10:19f. (with variants) and Luke 21:14f. In the time of trial a disciple will be inspired by God's (holy) spirit. Purity of heart is the harvest of God's presence and power, in those who have been baptized with the spirit through the ministry of Jesus (cf. Mark 1:8; Ps. 51:10f.).

> In all this Jesus was in marked agreement with Qumran piety and with the wisdom of others in the Judaism of his own time. This is neither surprising nor disquieting, for we should expect nothing less from one who was a son of the Law and the Prophets.

The conquest of vice, then, does not depend on moral effort and self-sufficiency, however much asking, seeking and knocking goes on. The proper petition is that of the Marcionite text of Luke 11:2, "let your holy spirit come upon us and purify us". To human aspiration and persistence must be added the encouragement of the divine spirit within, first of all for Jesus the Master himself, and next for his disciples. In John's words, *God is the Paraclete* who comforts, consoles, strengthens and protects those who represent him in the world, whatever their problems, sufferings, perplexities and battles in his cause. (The classical expression of this is in John 14-16.)

VI. RESURRECTION IN DISCIPLESHIP

The teaching of Jesus on discipleship liberates both the interpreter and the student from a false or exaggerated emphasis on the so-called eschatological dimension of his outlook, that is, one based on expectations of an imminent end to the physical world.

The doctrine means for women as well as men that God the Creator and Judge of all life and conduct is, was and ever shall be the holy, transcendent One, whose best name is *Abba,* a Sovereign who is also a Lover. Jesus claimed, and the Church still claims, that God's redemptive purpose was embodied in Jesus of Nazareth.

Some part of the truth had been glimpsed already during the odyssey of Israel through other prophets sent by God, but it became poignantly luminous in the fate of Jesus the Galilean prophet who called on the *Abba* in Gethsemane yet was not delivered from the agony of crucifixion.

In the human experience of Jesus, moral duty was continually illuminated by communion with God, and his staying power was similarly derived from God. In him, God provided for Israel a new "opening" in history; but not through apocalyptic wonders, nor by the convocation of an end-times court of judgement. When Jesus came into Galilee there came judgment and succour (a phrase I owe to Professor Herbert Farmer of Cambridge), but not of course the Last Judgment. It was God's gracious will to make a new beginning, Jesus taught; and those who had the insight to see this, and the faith to hear it, believed and turned afresh to God.

In one sense, it is true, Judgement came to the door; in another sense, it was a summons to a crusade in a new historical epoch.

The inauguration of that epoch was like seed quietly sown, like leaven ceaselessly at work (Q-Luke 13:18-21). The revelation came to the babes (Q-Luke 10:21). Its only sign was that of Jonah, an unlikely prophet sent by God to proclaim to an unlikely city the gospel of faith and returning (Q-Luke 11:29b).

Indeed, the Jesus-event was something greater than Jonah's preaching to Nineveh, something more pregnant with fateful meaning than the pilgrimage of the Queen of Sheba to the court of King

Solomon (Q-Luke 11:31). For in the life of Christ, God himself came on pilgrimage to Galilee, Judaea and Samaria.

But the prophet in whom his spirit dwelt would not and did not escape a prophet's fate. The ethic appropriate to one who ventured to represent God's holy purity and loving care had to be tied to an expectation of passion and death. It ought never to be isolated from the whole gospel that Jesus communicated in the manner of his life and dying.

This moral teaching was no mere outline of an interim discipline before the real Advent and Arrival of God, as Albert Schweitzer seems to have thought. The Rule of the new age was truly inaugurated, though not completed, in history. Jesus delineated by his words and acts the kind of life to be lived by his disciples, and by the company of believers who were to be converted by the testimony of those disciples after his death.

Nor was this an ideal for a realm of grace in the age to come, at the End of history. It was a realistic and quite uncompromising demand for discipline in the imitation of God. It left open the probability—for faith the certainty—that the God of the living has more in store for us, in life beyond death (Mark 12:26f.).

Jesus' teaching about virtue and vice, about purity of heart, loyalty, love of neighbour and love of enemy, stands or falls with the credibility of his theology and with the integrity that took him to death. In the churches for which the Synoptic Gospels were produced, being Christian meant to be a disciple of that same Jesus, it meant assuming a yoke that was easy only when the grace of God, revealed in Jesus and communicated through him, provided the criteria by which everything was judged; and only when spiritual power was poured out to enable the faithful to live graciously day by day.

BIBLIOGRAPHY

Page numbers are noted below when specific reference has been made to this material in the prededing text.

Israel Abrahams, *Studies in Pharisaism and the Gospels, 1,* reprint, Ktav, New York: 1967 (pages 19f.).

Gustaf Aulén *Jesus in Contemporary Historical Research,* Fortress Press, Philadelphia: 1976 (pages 135-163).

Kenneth Bailey, *Poet and Peasant,* Eerdmans, Grand Rapids: 1976.

Herbert Braun, *Jesus of Nazareth: The Man and His Time,* Fortress Press, Philadelphia: 1979

Earl Breech, "Kingdom of God and the Parables of Jesus" in *The Poetics of Faith, Semeia 12* (December 1978), Scholars Press, Chico, Calif. (pp, 15-40).

Rudolf Bultmann, *The History of the Synoptic Tradition,* Basil Blackwell, Oxford: 1968 (page 103).

Emily Carr, *Hundreds and Thousands: The Journals of Emily Carr,* Clarke Irwin & Co., Toronto/Vancouver: 1966 (page 34).

B. D Chilton, "Regnum Dei Deus Est", in *Scottish Journal of Theology,* vol. 31, no. 3 (1978) (pp. 261-70).

J. D. Crossan, *The Dark Interval,* Argus Communications, Niles, Ill.: 1975 (pages 101-104, 122).

C. H. Dodd, *The Parables of the Kingdom,* Scribners, New York: 1961.

R. A. Edwards, *The Theology of Q,* Fortress Press, Philadelphia: 1975.

David Flusser, *Jesus,* Herder and Herder, New York: 1969.

Michael Goulder, "Jesus, the Man of Universal Destiny" in *The Myth of God Incarnate,* John Hick, ed., S.C.M., London: 1977 (pages 48-63).

David Hill, *Matthew* (New Century Bible), Oliphants, 1972

A. M. Hunter, *A Pattern for Life,* Westminster Press, Philadelphia: 1953.

Joachim Jeremias, *The Lord's Prayer,* Fortress Press, Philadelphia: 1964 (pages 10-13).

R. G. Hamerton-Kelly, *God the Father: Theology and Patriachy in the Teaching of Jesus,* University Press, Cambridge: 1979.

James D. Kilpatrick, *The Origins of the Gospel According to Saint Matthew,* Clarendon Press, Oxford: 1946 (pages 25f.).

Hans Küng, *On Being a Christian,* Doubleday, Garden City NY: 1976.

Robert Kysar, *The Fourth Evangelist and his Message,* Augsburg, Minneapolis, Minn.: 1975.

T. W. Manson, (with Major and Wright), *The Mission and Message of Jesus,* Ivor Nicholson and Watson, London: 1937 (page 370).

Howard Marshall, ed., *New Testament Interpretation,* Eerdmans, Grand Rapids: 1977 (pp. 139-195).

C. G. Montefiore, *The Synoptic Gospels, II,* McMillan, London: (pages 29f.).

Eric Osborn, *Ethical Patterns in Early Christian Thought,* University Press, Cambridge: 1976 (pages 23, 191-198).

N. Perrin, *Rediscovering the Teaching of Jesus,* Harper and Row, New York and Evanston: 1967 (pages 52, 72f.).

J. Reumann, *Jesus in the Church's Gospels,* Fortress Press, Philadelphia: 1968.

J. T. Sanders, *Ethics in The New Testament,* Fortress Press, Philadelphia: 1975.

W. Schrage, "Ethics in the New Testament" in *Interpreter's Dictionary of the Bible,* Supplementary Volume, ed. Keith Crim, Abingdon, Nashville: 1976.

E. F. Scott, *The Fourth Gospel: its Purpose and Theology,* T. & T. Clark, Edinburgh: 1906 (page 65).

K. Stendahl, "Matthew" in *Peake's Commentary,* ed. Black and Rowley, Thos. Nelson and Sons, London: 1962 (page 780).

Paul Tillich, *The New Being,* Charles Scribner's Sons, New York: 1965 (page 32).

Scripture quotations are sometimes taken from the New English Bible (N.E.B.), the Good News Bible (Today's English Version or T.E.V.), and the Revised Standard Version, but frequently I have used my own translations.

DISCOVERING DISCIPLESHIP

A study guide of six sessions

by James Taylor

OVERVIEW
FOR LEADERS

These six sessions follow a consistent pattern. There is an opening, a time for input, a time for discussion, and a conclusion.

PREPARATION: Before beginning any of the sessions, you will need some preparation.

There is, first, *preparation of yourself.* You need to read thoroughly the materials in this book for each session, and to look up the scripture references and become familiar with them. If possible, read related materials recommended in the text; check available Bible commentaries, dictionaries, and encyclopedias. In going through these sources, look for similarities and differences, for ideas that strike sparks off each other. When you find yourself getting excited about your learning, others are more likely to become excited too.

Second, there is *preparation of others.* Any good program is the result of teamwork. A one-person performance may be impressive, but it often creates passive learners. By comparison, active learners learn faster and better because they are doing the learning themselves. So involve others as much as possible, in preparation and in leadership. A multitude of tasks need doing. These include:
—setting up the room or rooms.
—looking after distribution of books or study materials, registering people, etc.
—supplying tea/coffee and cookies, if desired.
—leading and guiding discussion in small groups.
—leading music or singing.
Make sure you have enough newsprint, if that's what you're using. And felt pens that write; chalk for a blackboard; a supply of pencils and paper if people are to write, etc.

SUPPLEMENTARY RESOURCES: Informed discussion is always preferable to a pooling of ignorance. The level of discussion and understanding will be significantly enhanced if all the participants can read and study this book. Other worthwhile books that are easily readable are:
Jesus Means Life, by Harold and Patricia Wells, published by the

Division of Communication of the United Church, $5.95
46 Images, by George Morrison, a book of daily devotions published by the Division of Mission in Canada, $3.95
William Neill's One Volume Bible Commentary, 8.50
An Everyday God, by James Taylor, published by Wood Lake Books, $5.95
The Parables of Jesus, by A.C. Forrest, published by Christian Journals, $8.95
The Gift of Story, by Ralph Milton, published by Wood Lake Books, $6.95
All of these are currently available from Canec Bookstores in Edmonton, Winnipeg, Toronto, and Dieppe, N.B.

A display of these books at the registration table, with encouragement to buy and read, will pay dividends during the study period.

Encourage participants and leaders to bring and use their own Bibles, especially during small group discussion periods.

The Session Pattern

OPENING: In this period, people need to start feeling comfortable with each other. Especially at the first session, participants are likely to feel uneasy, even though they may have known each other for a long time. In each session, use some appropriate group-building method to help people introduce themselves to each other.

The singing of some new and/or familiar songs works well in groups of a dozen or more; in smaller groups, an opportunity for intentional but informal conversation may be preferable.

Asking people to talk with someone else about buying their first pair of shoes, to tell a story about something in their wallet or purse, or about learning to ride a bicycle, or even to use various ways of introducing themselves may seem pointless but helps to reduce inhibitions people may have about discussing their faith with others.

In the first session, this period should probably take up to 20 minutes. In later sessions, less time will be necessary. To some extent, however, it is always needed when people gather.

ALTERNATIVE OPENING: George Johnston believes that an essential element in Bible study is worship. If that format is chosen, the opening period of each session could be devoted to a short worship service.

Use a worship pattern that is familiar to the participants, as in their customary Sunday service, up to the sermon.

The familiarity of the liturgy, and the inclusion of one or more familiar hymns, will effectively create much the same "breathing space" as other opening exercises, giving participants an opportunity to set aside other concerns and to focus on their study of scripture.

Since this option follows more-or-less accustomed worship practices, it has not been elaborated each time in the individual session plans.

INPUT: In general, take 15 to 20 minutes for this part of the meeting. If the alternative worship-opening is used, this input period would replace a sermon or meditation.

A key in encouraging learning on the part of others is to share your own learning. Tell how your own understanding may have been affected or changed in your preparation for this session. Acknowledge where you have difficulties with the material, as well as where you are in agreement.

Do not simply read or repeat Dr. Johnston's ideas verbatim. Rather, put those ideas into your own words, illustrating them from your own experience. Ralph Milton's *Gift of Story* explains why this method is effective.

DISCUSSION: If there are no more than a dozen in the study group, there may be no need to divide into smaller groups. With larger numbers, it is better to divide into groups of six to eight, to enable all to participate more fully.

Discussion groups need leaders. Do not leave leadership to chance. In advance, choose people who can keep the discussion on the general theme, while neither allowing it to wander aimlessly nor arbitrarily restricting it to narrow limits. Talk over the session's theme and purpose with them, so that they know what is expected of them.

The questions listed for each session are suggestions only. Sometimes an apparently silly question evokes the most penetrating response! Use these questions when they work; ignore them when they don't; substitute your own questions and struggles or those of the small group leaders when it seems appropriate.

This part of the program will almost always require at least 30 minutes. If discussion goes well, groups may want up to an hour. But do not continue past an hour—it's better to quit while people still want more.

CLOSING: If you have several small groups, serving coffee and/or tea and cookies provides some unorganized time for people to gather. Allow up to 15 minutes for this process.

If you have just one group, coffee may be more appropriate at the beginning or the end of the session.

Once participants are back in to a single large group, ask for the insights or questions that may have developed during the preceding discussion. The basic concern in this period is: "What have you learned from tonight's discussion?" In some situations, 10 minutes may be more than sufficient for this part of the program; if the discussion has stimulated serious thinking, however, it may be necessary to allow 20 minutes or more.

Conclude with:
—instructions for preparation for the next session;
—music or singing if appropriate.
—prayer. Encourage lay persons to lead in prayer as part of their growth in discipleship.

If the opening of the session is treated as worship, this part of the session should be similarly treated as the conclusion of worship, including a dismissal with a blessing or benediction. For the final session, participants may wish to share in an informal celebration of the Lord's Supper.

VENTURES IN MISSION

VENTURES IN MISSION is a national program of the United Church of Canada, established in response to needs expressed by congregations and presbyteries.

Its goal is the spiritual renewal of United Church congregations, in co-operation with other programs. An improved understanding of stewardship and discipleship will provide long-term benefits for the people of the church. To this end, the whole church is encouraged to take part in a program of Information and Study during 1983.

The financial goal of VENTURES IN MISSION is to raise $40 million in a special appeal culminating in 1984. Some $16 million is intended for the development of new communities of faith, according to needs identified by the Conferences of the United Church; $9 million for church re-development, revitalizing churches struggling to fulfill their mission in changed environments; and $15 million to refinance part of the Pension Plan which currently requires a subsidy of some $2 million a year from the Mission and Service Fund.

Leaders of groups should be aware of the aims of VENTURES IN MISSION, and could encourage recognition and support of this program when it seems appropriate in the discussions.

This study has been produced in the conviction that, as the VENTURES Statement of Mission puts it: "We believe that we are called to search, struggle, and work together to discern the ways of faithfulness, following a vision which provides no easy answers but leads us in paths of hope and renewal."

SESSION PLANS

SESSION ONE:
The Kingdom Comes

PURPOSE: To explore the meaning of "The Kingdom of God" as a time when God's will is done.

PREPARATION: For this session, the applicable sections are:
in Part 1, pages 12-16,
in Part II, pages 17-20,
in Part IV, pages 39-40.

In general, Dr. Johnston states that Jesus came preaching about the coming of the Kingdom. But it was not a kingdom such as the world knows, where kings rule autocratically. Nor was it a heavenly kingdom removed from this world, nor even the end of this world, though that claim is still often heard today. For Jesus, the Kingdom is a reality in which people understand God's will and give it highest priority in their daily lives.

In this session, people need to understand what Jesus meant by the Kingdom and to begin some searching to discern God's will at the present time.

The first chapter of *Jesus Means Life,* and sections in *46 Images* on King, Kingdom, and Servant may provide helpful insights.

OPENING: Welcome the participants. Introduce the leadership team and the course of study.

Use an appropriate group-building method to help people introduce themselves to each other.

Take up to 20 minutes to make sure that people feel comfortable with each other before proceeding into serious discussion.

INPUT: Use a passage such as Mark 1:14-15 to present the theme of the coming of the Kingdom. Remember that this is not a time to win converts to the Kingdom—or to the speaker's own idea of what the Kingdom is—but to help participants explore what Jesus meant by the Kingdom.

DISCUSSION: Small groups should focus on the question of the Kingdom as our doing as well as God's. If the Kingdom really is a matter of understanding and doing God's will as our top priority, then the coming of the Kingdom depends on our initiative, and not simply on a divine decree.

You might ask:
• if God is almighty, why was it necessary to give us minds?
• if you were told the Kingdom was coming at 8:02 tomorrow morning (or any other specific time) what would you do? Why aren't you doing that now? What did Jesus' hearers do?
• how can we discover what God's will really is? Why are there so many differences of opinion about it?
• what might we, here and now, be doing to use our talents and resources to further God's will?

CLOSING: Find out what people have learned from tonight's discussion.

In preparation for next week, read:
—in Part II: pages 20-22,
—in Part III: pages 29-30 (Humility), 36-38 (Purity).

Conclude with music and/or prayer.

SESSION TWO:
To Represent Jesus

PURPOSE: To explore the duty of disciples to represent Jesus, as Jesus represented God.

PREPARATION: Read:
in Part II: pages 20-22,
in Part III: pages 29-30 (Humility), 36-38 (Purity).

In summary, Dr. Johnston asserts that Jesus by his presence ushered in a new age, the Kingdom which is "within reach", "among" or "in the midst of you". He sent out his disciples to represent him to all whom they met, just as he represented the personality and nature of God. This "apostolic impersonation" continues to be our task today.

OPENING: Welcome the participants from the last session; introduce any new people who may have joined the gathering. Through music or other activities, encourage mixing and getting acquainted.

INPUT: The sending out of the disciples, in Luke 10:1-16, might be a good basis for consideration of this topic. Remember that the point here is not so much the kinds of things that Jesus instructed the disciples to do, as that they went out with the responsibility of "being Jesus" for others.

DISCUSSION: This subject may evoke two different theologies among the participants: those who see Jesus as primarily human, and therefore one who can be emulated; and those who see him as primarily divine, and therefore beyond human attainment. Dr. George Morrison's book, 46 Images, has some helpful insights into the differences that result from perceptions of Jesus as "Son of Man" and "Son of God".

Some questions to stimulate discussion are:
• How is the authority/responsibility for representing Jesus passed on?
• To follow Jesus' example, do we have to wear sandals in the middle of winter?
• Does representing Jesus have to be on a face-to-face basis?
• Jesus deliberately spent time with the poor and powerless and outcasts of Jewish society. At least in the early days of his ministry, he was also a regular attender and often speaker in synagogues, so he may have spent significant amounts of time among middle-class God-fearing people much like Canadian Christians. To whom should we be representing Jesus today?

CLOSING: Ask for insights or concerns that may have developed during this session's discussion.

Assign the reading or preparation for next session:
—in Part III, pages 25 (Obedience) -30
Close with music/prayer.

SESSION THREE:
Four Character Qualities

PURPOSE: To begin looking at the specific qualities of personality that are required of a disciple.

PREPARATION: In the book, read the following:
—in Part III, pages 25-30 (Obedience-Humility).

Although many qualities could have been cited, Dr. Johnston concentrates on a few: trust, loyalty, humility, obedience. Significantly, some qualities that might be valued today have been omitted, such as initiative, courage, leadership, etc. The emphasis is on discerning and fulfilling God's will, and avoiding anything that could be distorted into the pursuit of one's own will.

OPENING: Sometimes an opening activity can be a means of introducing the theme. In this instance, people might pair off, and for three minutes, tell each other about a quality in the other person that they admire. Or they might identify a favorite movie star/television personality/business leader/etc., and explain why that person is admired.

INPUT: Although the dominant and recurring theme throughout this book is obedience, any of the qualities listed could form the basis for presentation of the theme. Choose the quality that most catches your own imagination, and proceed from there.

Remember that these concepts are more likely to come alive if you can use personal experiences to illustrate how trust, loyalty, humility, or obedience are essential qualities of discipleship.

DISCUSSION: It will probably not be possible to cover in depth all four qualities in this one session. If possible, keep the discussion centred on why Jesus wanted those qualities in his disciples, rather than exhaustively analyzing any one quality.

Suggested questions:
• If you were hiring someone for a long-term and often unsupervised job, what qualities would you look for?
• Can you be proud of being humble?
• Is God looking for dedicated "fools" who will rush in where smarter "angels" fear to tread?
• Where and what are the needs today that might be calling for our trust, loyalty, humility, and obedience?

CLOSING: The best summary of learnings may come in the practical needs uncovered by the final question. Ask people to call out these needs, whether or not they completed discussing that question in groups. List their comments on newsprint or a blackboard, so that all can see.

The list itself may generate further discussion, as some people perceive needs that others had missed or overlooked.

Assign reading for next session:
—in Part III, pages 23-25.
Close with prayer/music.

SESSION FOUR:
Vision and Insight

PURPOSE: To recognize that a vital function of disciples is to be able to see what others cannot see and hear what others cannot hear.

PREPARATION: Read, in the text, the following section:
—in Part III, pages 23-25.

Part of the vision that Jesus expected of his disciples was an ability to see in the commonplace and everyday things of their lives the evidence and the message of God. Most significantly, they were to see in the life and person of Jesus himself, an ordinary mortal to those lacking this vision and insight, the divine presence of God.

This theme is a primary focus of *An Everyday God,* by James Taylor, published by Wood Lake Books and available through Canec.

OPENING: To set the stage for the input period, you might use an activity whose only purpose is to encourage people to look for and ask about things they have never previously considered.

For example, give each person a list of such items as: color of hair, color of eyes, month of birth, shoe size, middle initial, etc. Have them fill in their own details—then have them find a "twin" among the group for each of their own characteristics, if possible.

INPUT: This theme could be developed using a variety of texts. Comment might focus on Mark 4:12 or the related passages that quote Isaiah 6:9-10, stresssing the inability of would-be disciples to see and hear beyond the particulars of their life to God's will. Alternatively, the positive side of being able to see and hear could be developed from Luke 10:23f.

Or, returning in part to the Kingdom theme of Session One, the text could be from Luke 17:20f., with the emphasis on the qualities of the Kingdom that make it invisible to eyes that are not accustomed to looking for it.

Or the theme could be developed through some of Jesus' shorter parables, such as those in Luke 13:18-25, in which Jesus may have selected the material for his messages from common scenes along the road.

DISCUSSION: People will probably recognize and be able to share a number of incidents in which others have failed to see God's presence in certain situations—being unaware of a caring community in the midst of grief, for example. It may be more difficult for them to recognize occasions when they may have been similarly unaware.

Questions that could be asked are:
• How do people learn to see universal truths in specific incidents?
• If you can't see invisible truths, should you visit a medium?
• Do we expect to hear from God only in extraordinary or unexplainable ways? Are we missing simple ordinary messages?
• What difference might it make in our lives and in our church if we had "the eyes to see and the ears to hear"? What might God be wanting us to see and hear today?

CLOSING: In gathering insights and understandings out of discussion in this session, ask especially about practical applications that could result from seeking to discern God's will in literally anything and everything. The key question for evaluating the learning in this session is the last one: "What difference might it make..."?

Assign reading for the next session:
—in Part III, pages 30 (Forgiveness) -36.
Conclude with prayer and/or music.

SESSION FIVE:
The Caring Neighbour

PURPOSE: To see that there are no exceptions or exclusions to Jesus' command to love others.

PREPARATION: Before the session, read:
—in Part III, pages 30-36.

You may also find it helpful to read through the opening chapters of *The Parables of Jesus,* by A.C. Forrest, especially "Those Infuriating Parables", and "The Good Samaritan".

Dr. Johnston suggests that Jesus' ethical teachings in the Sermon on the Mount call us to impossible standards, in which anger, lust, and revenge are completely excluded. The parable of the Good Samaritan shows how that standard of behaviour may be expressed in practice, but raises the added problems of God's will being demonstrated by those who are despised and rejected. The Golden Rule provides a principle underlying both the teachings and the parable.

In preparing for this session's input, do not get diverted into arguments about what Jesus did or did not say. Rather, concentrate on the significance of the selected passages.

OPENING: To introduce the theme, you might have people pair off and tell each other for a couple of minutes about strangers: experiences with them, perhaps experiences of being a stranger, what they teach their children about strangers, etc.

INPUT: The text, if one is used, should probably be the Golden Rule (Luke 6:31). The parable of the Good Samaritan and the excerpts from Matthew's version of the Sermon on the Mount could then become illustrations and examples.

Remember that these teachings were not given by Jesus as laws, but as ideals. If these teachings are treated as laws, two results are likely: 1) they will be shrugged off by mere mortals as impossible, and 2) efforts to enforce them as laws will require emphasis on the eternal and inevitable punishment awaiting the lawbreakers, rather than on God's love and compassion. Rather, focus on Jesus himself, who personified in his life the qualities expected from his disciples. Recall the emphasis in Session Two on disciples as "apostolic impersonators" of Jesus.

DISCUSSION: Questions could be:
• How often do the TV programs and commercials you watch contradict Jesus' teachings against anger, lust, swearing, revenge, and hostility?
• What good is a law if you can't enforce it?
• Are there any habits of dress, food, behaviour, social or ethnic qualities in other people that you find intolerable? How about immigrants, people with mental or physical disabilities, criminals, etc.?
• Who might be a "Jericho road victim" in need of help today? Are more people "beaten up and left to die" by economic injustice—such as inflation, expropriation, arbitrary policies, and impersonal large scale projects—than by physical violence?

CLOSING: After hearing some of the insights developed in the discussion period, take the final question one step further. Ask what people or groups may be looking for assistance, not from governments or some nebulous other source, but specifically from the churches. Have people call out their ideas, and list them on newsprint or on a blackboard, without getting into intense discussion about any of the suggestions.

Assign reading for the last session:
—in Part III, pages 36-38 (Purity),
—in Part IV, pages 39-40.
Conclude with prayer and/or music, as usual.

SESSION SIX:
The Fruit of the Tree

PURPOSE: To see that the proof of discipleship is demonstrated by one's actions in life.

PREPARATION: Read the following sections:
—in Part III, pages 36-38
—in Part IV, pages 39-40.

The theme here is stated by George Johnston: "Piety must conform to the character of the God who is worshipped; behaviour must fit the goodness of the same God." Leviticus 19:2 gives a similar admonition: "You shall be holy because I, the Lord your God, am holy" (N.E.B.). To assess a disciple's character, the heart and motivations must be searched; the evidence of the pure heart is revealed by a person's actions.

If the group wishes to conclude with a brief communion service, arrangements for bread and wine, for music and servers, need to be made in advance.

OPENING: Whatever is done during this period should be fairly brief, as the closing is likely to take longer than usual.

INPUT: In addition to the passages from Mark and Luke referred to in the text, the commentary could be based on the New Testament letter of James 1:23-25, or 2:14-18. For clarity in the second passage, a newer translation such as the *Good News* or *New English Bible* is recommended.

Remember that this is the last session. If what the participants have been learning is to result in any commitment to discipleship—financially or socially, internally or as outreach to others, as individuals or as a group—that commitment must grow out of this session.

DISCUSSION: Some questions to stimulate discussion are:
• Do people ever deliberately choose to do wrong?
• How does a tree put forth bad fruit? What can be done about the fruit? About the tree?
• When you're troubled by some shortcoming or omission, does it tend to poison everything else that you do?
• What opportunities are open to us to show our faith by our works in this time when government-funded programs take care of most people's basic health and housing necessities?

Participants should be aware that VENTURES IN MISSION may be one of those opportunities without having that choice imposed on them.

CLOSING: It is important to give participants a chance to reflect on the whole series of study sessions. One way of doing this is to ask them to complete on a piece of paper or a file card sentences such as the following:
—What I liked best about these sessions was......................
—I wish that we had..
—I learned that..
Collect these responses for evaluation later by the leadership team.

From the fifth session, bring out the list that was made of those who may be looking to this group for assistance. See if there are new suggestions to be added to the list—especially any that may be related to the VENTURES IN MISSION objectives (see page 49).

Suggest that if these study sessions have made any difference, the new understanding of discipleship needs to bear fruit; it needs to be affirmed and confirmed by a commitment to action.

Ask the group how they feel about taking action together. If there is a consensus, try to have them select from the list one or more projects that they can support, or that they may want to recommend to the congregation for support.

If there is no consensus, invite each person to choose from the list one area of need to which he or she will try to respond in discipleship. Have the members of the group write their choices down on individual pieces of paper, privately, as a covenant between themselves and God.

Choose a couple of people to be responsible for destroying these papers in due course, without breaking confidentiality. Collect the papers on an offering plate.

To integrate this process with the concluding communion, the plate of papers can be brought forward and presented at the same time as the elements of communion are brought in and presented.

The breaking of bread and the sharing of the wine may follow any accepted tradition. The *Service Book for the Use of Ministers* includes a simple form of the Celebration of the Lord's Supper, suggested for use in house churches and small groups.

Conclude with a hymn, a commissioning to discipleship, and a benediction.